MY CULTURE

YORUBA

A QUICK GUIDE TO
YORUBA CULTURE FOR
BRITISH TEACHERS

FLORENCE OLAJIDE

Matador
9 Priory Business Park
Kibworth Beauchamp
Leicestershire LE8 0RX, UK
Tel: (+44) 116 279 2299
Fax: (+44) 116 279 2277
Email: books@troubador.co.uk
Web: www.troubador.co.uk/matador

ISBN 978 1780880 716

British Library Cataloguing in Publication Data.
A catalogue record for this book is available from the British Library.

Typeset in 12pt Bembo by Troubador Publishing Ltd, Leicester, UK
Printed and bound in the UK by TJ International, Padstow, Cornwall

Matador is an imprint of Troubador Publishing Ltd

To all the family and friends who have accepted me just as I am.

CONTENTS

vii

PREFACE

The Black African ethnic group is probably one of the fastest growing minority groups in Britain today. This population growth has been influenced by several factors, notably immigration and a higher child birth rate. British schools have worked with Black and minority ethnic groups for decades. The high concentration of these groups in large cities, such as London and Birmingham, has meant that inner city schools have developed a wealth of knowledge and understanding about them. However, in recent years, upward social mobility has meant that more Black African families have begun to move into the suburbs. For schools in these areas, this has meant a significant change in clientele in a relatively short period of time. Consequently, many are ill-equipped to deal with the cultural issues surrounding the needs of such children and their families.

The aim of this book, therefore, is to provide a quick introduction to Yoruba culture, from which the majority of Black African children living in the UK originate. Children from minority ethnic backgrounds see the world differently. On a daily basis, their behaviours and actions are filtered through at least two, and sometimes more, cultural filters. For children of Yoruba descent living in the UK, the cultures in question are diametrically opposing in nature. On a mental level, this requires children to process a wider range of information and emotions than the norm, when dealing with day-to-day situations. Often, it also requires behaviour that is at opposite extremes, which, in turn, may result in internal conflict on an emotional level. I refer to this process as cultural conflict. As an individual born in Britain but of Yoruba parents, I have personally experienced many of the issues described in this book, as indeed have several family members. Caught between two opposing worlds, I would describe my personal road to self-discovery as long and painful, yet the same experiences are being recreated in the lives of hundreds of children in our society today.

By writing this book, I hope to shed some light on some of the struggles bi-cultural children face as a result of cultural conflict. The book is designed to provide some quick insights into the psyche of Yoruba culture and to explain some day-to-day issues that teachers and educators may face when dealing with children and families from the culture group. It also explains some of the ramifications of cultural conflict in the life experiences of Yoruba children, and suggests some ideas for minimising any negative impact. I hope that readers will find it a useful guide and introduction to the world of culture learning.

A word of warning: by their very nature, discussions about culture invariably involve making generalisations, which in turn are prone to stereotyping. The information provided in this book is born out of personal knowledge and experience. Nonetheless, it is not intended to be the definitive word on Yoruba culture. There will be exceptions to the rule and readers should not take the information provided as applicable to every Yoruba person or family they meet.

UNDERSTANDING YORUBA CULTURE

Chapter 1:

An Introduction to Yoruba Cultural Origins, Language and Religion

Ọmọ ilẹ̀ Odùdúwà, ọmọ ilẹ̀ káǎrọ̀, ojíre

(A child of the land of Oduduwa, of the land where we say 'good morning, did you sleep well?')

Yoruba people can be found all over the world, but they live mainly in the south western parts of Nigeria and in some parts of Togo and the Benin Republic in West Africa. The Yoruba have lived in West Africa for centuries. They believe that they descend from a common ancestor called Oduduwa, who was the first king of a Yoruba city called Ile-Ife. Oduduwa is believed to have had several sons who founded other Yoruba city states, such as Owu, Ketu, Ila, Sabe, Popo, Ilesha, Ondo and Oyo. The Yoruba also believe that the ancient city of Benin, in Nigeria, was founded by a son of Oduduwa.

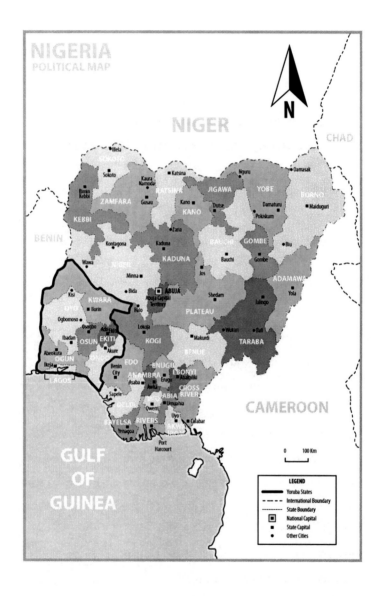

The Yoruba city states, which formed the capitals of each Yoruba tribe, were known for highly centralised and complex forms of government, often with a monarch called an *Oba* at the helm. City states differed in the degree to which their kings were absolute monarchs, and some states operated a degree of democracy with a council of elders who were elected and worked together with the king to create a balance of power. The kings of each town or city often have a specific title. The king of Ile-Ife, known as the *Ooni* of Ife, was, and still is, regarded as the most senior of all the Yoruba kings. Each tribe spoke a different dialect of the Yoruba language until the second half of the nineteenth century, when Samuel Ajayi Crowther, a freed slave and the first African Bishop of the Church of England, translated the language into English. He also published a Yoruba grammar and parts of the Bible. Through Crowther's work, a standard form of the language was created and is now used in written form and taught at school.

The Yoruba Language

The Yoruba language is tonal with three levels of tone: high, mid and low. The acute accent (´) depicts the high tone and the grave accent (`) depicts the low tone. Syllables with a mid tone are often left unmarked but sometimes the macron (¯) is used to show this. Every syllable has a tone and these are used to distinguish between words that are spelt exactly the same but with different meanings. Hence **Sókótó** (a city in one of the northern states of Nigeria) is distinguished from **Sòkòtò** (a pair of trousers), and depending on the accents, *Ogun* can mean one of seven things: war, medicine, strife, sweat, twenty, inheritance or the god of iron. In everyday use, however, it is not uncommon for people to miss out the accents, as meaning can often be derived from the context in which a word is used.

Standard Yoruba uses the Latin alphabet and consists of twenty five letters.

A	B	D	E	Ẹ	F	G	Gb	H	I	J	K	L	M	N	O	Ọ	P	R	S	Ṣ	T	U	W	Y
a	b	d	e	ẹ	f	g	gb	h	i	j	k	L	m	n	o	ọ	p	r	s	ṣ	t	u	w	y

The Latin letters C, Q, V, X and Z are not used. Diacritics underneath the letters E and O are used to depict the open vowels: /ɛ/ as in **pet** and /ɒ/ as in **pot**. Most of the other letters are pronounced as one would, using the International Phonetic Alphabet. There are some notable exceptions. The letter **Ṣ** represents the English digraph /**sh**/. The letters **P** and **Gb** are labial-velar stops, pronounced with a plosive sound and have no equivalents in the English alphabet. They are pronounced simultaneously with the lips, with the back of the tongue pressed against the soft palate and with air flowing out of the mouth only.

The Yoruba language is very descriptive and many modern nouns in the English language would have a Yoruba equivalent which is an adjective. For example, 'aeroplane' in Yoruba is *Ọkọ̀ Òfúrufú*, which translated means 'the vehicle that moves in the sky'. The language is also rich in idioms, sayings and proverbs, many of which indicate the core norms and values of Yoruba society. Accordingly, the Yoruba have an apt saying for almost every life circumstance you can imagine.

Modes of Communication

Prior to the written form of the language being established, most of the culture was passed down from generation to generation through word of mouth, folklore and songs. The Yoruba people, like many Africans, are effusive in their communication. British people can

7

sometimes find this overpowering. The heavy use of gestures and the waving of hands is a normal part of the body language and communication tends to be much louder than the Western European norm. This is very noticeable at social functions where music is played at very high decibels, while people's conversations continue undisturbed. Most teachers in British schools will find that Yoruba children, when distressed or excited, may become somewhat theatrical, compared to the British norm, that is, in their body language and use of voice.

Religion

Christianity and Islam are the main religions practised by the Yoruba. However, in pre-colonial times, animism was practised and the Yoruba worshiped several deities. This practice persists today in many communities and families. Animism also bred superstitions and, although it is no longer the main form of religion, many superstitions have been handed down from generation to generation and are still firmly believed today. The Yoruba are generally tolerant of religious difference and it is not unusual for families to have Christian and Muslim members who coexist peaceably.

Yoruba Names

Many Yoruba family names are derived from the different deities that are worshiped. Names that start with *Ògún* (god of iron and war), *Ṣàngó* (god of thunder), *Ọya* (river goddess), *Ifá* or *Odù* (god of wisdom and divination) reflect this. Other names may reflect family professions, personal or family circumstances or express thanks and worship to God. Names starting with *Ọdẹ* reflect a warrior background, those starting with *Ọlá* reflect wealth and those starting with *Adé* reflect royalty or links with the ruling class.

The naming of a new born is an important rite of passage in Yoruba tradition. Traditionally boys would be named on the ninth day following their birth and girls on the seventh. In modern times all babies are named on the eighth day. The names given to children are meant to reflect the circumstances surrounding their birth. First names are divided into two categories, those that are predestined, *Orúkọ Àmútọrunwá*, meaning 'the name brought from heaven', and natural names, *Orúkọ Àbísọ*. Predestined names reflect natural circumstances, such as twins named *Táiwò* (contracted form of *Táyéwò*), meaning 'came to taste the world', and *Kẹhìndé*, meaning 'came last' (given to the second twin born). Yoruba people believe in reincarnation, so a male child born after the death of a grandfather would be named *Babátúndé*, meaning 'father has come back'. Similarly, a female child born after the death of a grandmother would be called *Yétúndé* or *Yéjídé*. Other predestined names include *Ìdòwú* and *Àlàbá* (the next two children born after a set of twins), *Abíódún* (born during a significant festival), and *Abósèdé* (born on a Sunday – first day of the week). All other natural names follow the usual naming conventions and may start with *Adé*, *Olá* or *Olú* (a contraction for God).

Yoruba Culture, Norms and Values

Like all societies, there are certain cultural norms and values that are important to the Yoruba people. One of the most important is respect for one's elders. Usually, being an elder is measured by chronological age, but not always. As such, elders could be one's superiors at work; pupils in a year group higher than yours at school; people with higher political authority or even wealth; and for a new wife in her husband's family, every adult and child (provided the children were able to walk independently at the wedding). Yoruba people also highly value good character and hard work. This is reflected in a popular saying: *Ìwà lẹwà*, meaning 'good character is synonymous with beauty'. A child's good behaviour is seen as a reflection of how well he or she has been raised and a badly behaved child is a disgrace to the family.

Greetings or felicitations are very important in Yoruba land, and an individual's ability to use and observe the appropriate greeting in any situation is seen as a measure of their good upbringing. Traditionally, when saying hello, younger females will kneel to greet their elders, while males will prostrate (lie face to the ground). In modern times and depending on social class, deep curtsying and bowing may be used as alternatives. However, during formal marriage transactions between families, only the traditional mode of greeting is acceptable. Yoruba people have a greeting for every possible circumstance; be it happy, sad or just mundane. Most greetings start with the words '*Ẹ kú*', for which there is no easy English translation. Apart from the standard ways of saying hello at specified times of the day, such as *Ẹkú àárọ̀* (good morning) or *Ẹkú ìrọ̀lẹ́* (good evening), depending on the situation, other greetings will express sympathy, empathy, commiserations or joy. So integral is this value to Yoruba culture, it is said that after the abolition of the slave trade in 1807, liberated slaves from Yoruba land who were repatriated to Freetown in Sierra Leone were called the *Aku* people (derived from *Ẹkú*) by the Europeans.

A well known saying, *Iṣẹ́ logùn iṣẹ*, meaning 'hard work is the panacea for poverty', shows how important the virtue of hard work is to the Yoruba person. As a result, Yoruba people are industrious and most, including those in paid employment, will engage in a number of other enterprising activities to earn additional money to support their immediate and extended families.

African Time

The notion of 'African time' is a well known one, suggesting that Africans are never punctual, at least not by British standards. Within a social context, this is certainly true of the Yoruba people. This is because the Yoruba believe that it is impolite to arrive at a social function early. It is implied that those who arrive too early do so in order to get to the food first and hence an indication of greed. As a result, 'fashionably late' takes on a new meaning as this could mean two or even three hours after the declared time on an invitation. Another reason why lateness is habitual among many Nigerians is the lack of a good public transport system. A shortage of sufficient buses to meet the needs of the public makes it almost impossible to predict when one might arrive at one's destination. As a result, over the decades, people have learnt to take a more laid-back approach to travelling and punctuality. Unfortunately, although such excuses do not exist in the British context, well-established habits are hard to break.

Chapter 2:

Attitudes to Power and Authority

Bí ọmọdé bá mọwọ́ wẹ̀, ábá àgbà jẹun

*(If children learn to wash their hands correctly, they will eat
with their elders)*

Yoruba culture is essentially autocratic, a leftover from pre-colonial days. Although in modern times governments have been democratically elected, the electoral processes and the discharge of governmental roles and responsibilities often fall back towards autocratic tendencies. The society is highly hierarchical, starting with the elders or rulers at the top, down to children at the bottom. This has a significant impact on social interaction. When relating to and addressing others, an individual must do so on the basis that the other person is either a superior, peer or subordinate. The concept of mutual respect is culturally unknown and respect is something one does in relation to one's superiors. When meeting someone else for the first time, a Yoruba person must quickly determine their own rank in relation to the other person. This is because, as a mark of respect, people must not call their superiors by their first name and usually must defer to them in matters of decision making. Also, to show respect, the plural form of the word 'you' must be used when addressing or referring to a superior. This rule is universal and operates at all levels of Yoruba society.

Within families, adults with children are referred to as the father or mother of their child. So Femi's father would be called **Bàbá Fẹ́mi** (the father of Femi) and his mother would be called **Màmá Fẹ́mi** (the mother of Femi). In pre-colonial times, younger siblings would refer to their older ones as **Ẹ̀gbọ́n,** meaning 'my older sibling'. In modern times, however, the culture has borrowed titles from the English language and words like sister, brother, auntie and uncle are used as a preface to people's names to avoid inappropriately calling them by their first names. In a sense, these words have become titles that identify rank within social interaction. Accordingly, most people will call their elders uncle, auntie, brother or sister, even though most of these would be no blood relation at all. In formal situations, particularly where it is more difficult to determine rank, in order to not cause offence, people will defer to one another by using official forms of address such as 'Mr' or 'Mrs' and by using the plural form of the word 'you'.

These cultural rules also apply to Yoruba children living in Britain. However, the culture does not insist that the rules be applied to non-Yoruba people, so Yoruba children learn the distinction between addressing elders within the culture group and those from other backgrounds. Some conflict can occur in families where parents are very traditional. For example, older siblings, conforming to the less formal British norm, may insist that their younger siblings call them by their first name, much to their parents' annoyance. In less traditional families, and where permission to do so has been granted, it is becoming more common for children to call their older siblings by their given names.

Decision making processes within families tend to be very autocratic and elders expect to be obeyed. Obeisance, particularly by children, is regarded as a virtue and parents expect to be able to influence the decisions made by their children throughout their life. British-born Nigerian youths often find this aspect of their parents' culture difficult to cope with. They may struggle with the notion that their parents do not *respect* them or their views as in the British way, and that they are not treated as independent young adults, especially when it comes to making choices about their future career or spouse.

Traditionally, work roles within society reflect clear divisions of labour. This has carried over to modern times, with professional jobs given higher status than jobs that are administrative or require manual labour. This is regardless of how lucrative the jobs may be. The use of job titles to show rank is a normal practice and, in addition to doctors, engineers and pastors, Yoruba people may use their professional titles to precede their name. Parents naturally want their children to enter the highest ranking professions and this may be another source of conflict, especially where the interests and aptitudes of a child do not match parental expectations.

When children start school, parents transfer their authority to the teachers and confer on them the right to discipline their children as they deem fit, but fairly.

Given the cultural views about respect and elders, parents also expect their children to obey their teachers as they would them. For Yoruba families living in Britain, this can be a source of cultural conflict. Having transferred their authority to teachers, parents do not expect to be significantly involved in issues relating to the management of their child's behaviour at school. In stark contrast, British schools expect parents to be significant partners with the school in their children's education. Serious behaviour infractions at school are usually reported to parents, who are expected to work with the school in resolving them. Parents may have signed a home-school agreement, as is the usual practice in British schools, indicating they would do so. However, they may not necessarily have the same understanding as the school of its significance or the school's expectation of them as parents.

The source of this confusion lies in the customary practice in Nigeria, of clear and more rigid divisions of labour and a tendency towards specialising within professions. While many people may combine their main professional career with some other form of enterprise, usually in the form of trading, it is rare for people to have more than one professional skill at the same time. This tendency towards specialism means that professionals are deemed experts in their fields and everyone else an amateur. Translated to education, this means that parents will view teachers as experts in schooling their children and are less likely to see themselves as equal partners in that process. They would therefore expect teachers, as experts, to be able to resolve behavioural issues which occur at school without their personal involvement. The issue of specialism also means that, although parents will encourage their children to complete their homework, they are less likely to take a 'hands on' approach to helping them with it. This does not mean that they do not care enough about their children's education. Many simply do not consider that they have sufficient expertise to provide their children with the right support. Indeed, many send their children to Saturday schools or employ teachers to support their children with homework in the evenings.

Generally speaking, when it comes to decisions about what happens in school, Nigerian and, in particular, Yoruba parents are more likely to defer to school officials. There are three notable exceptions to this generalisation, namely issues to do with children's future career choices, managing behaviour at home and matters pertaining to educating children with special educational needs. These three areas will be discussed in more detail in the following chapters.

Chapter 3:

Family and Social Structures

Ènìyàn lașọ

(People around you should cover and protect you like clothes)

At its core, Yoruba culture is collectivist in nature. There is a strong belief in the interdependence of every member of the community and the needs of the collective take priority over those of the individual. This core value has a significant impact on interpersonal interactions and is reflected in the saying *Àgbájọ ọwọ́ lafi nsọ̀yá,* meaning 'you need your whole hand to beat your chest'. In other words, all members of the community need to work together to be effective.

In pre-colonial times, the economy of the Yoruba states was predominantly agricultural and for economical reasons families tended to be on the large side. Polygamy was practised with no limit on the number of wives a man could take. Families often lived in large compounds which would include several scions of the extended family. In modern times, the nuclear family size has reduced to an average of four children. While polygamy is still practised, it is no longer common among Christian and educated families. Western influence, class and education levels have created significant variances in the social structures and behaviours within Yoruba families. Nonetheless, the interdependence upon one another remains as strong a cultural trait as it has ever been, and the extended family plays a prominent role in the life of each individual.

One of the reasons why the culture of interdependence has remained strong is because there is no state welfare system in Nigeria. This function is carried out through extended family networks which operate on a collective basis to help family members in need, whatever the need. Poorer family members will often go to live with richer ones. In exchange for food and board, the poorer relative will provide domestic services such as cleaning and cooking. If the poorer relative is a child, the richer family will often take on all the responsibility of seeing the child through adulthood. This will include covering the cost of their education and their eventual marriage. It is also the duty and responsibility of all extended family members to contribute towards the cost of large social functions, in particular funerals and weddings. This ensures important rites of passage are carried out regardless of the individual's financial situation.

Given the importance of family, key social events such as funerals and weddings require the attendance of all family members wherever possible. Absence from such events is seen as a personal slight. This often puts pressure on parents living in Britain to take their children out of school during term time to attend these functions. Even if schools feel they are not able to authorise such absences, it is important that they understand the social significance of such events for the family.

To maintain the above norms, people are encouraged to work together and individuals are pressured to conform to group ideals. Individuals who try to assert their individuality and break away from the norm are seen as a danger to the well-being and safety of the group, as their behaviour could encourage others to become dissidents. Therefore, whenever the well-being of the group is perceived to be at risk, the extended family will act as a unifying force and exert strong overt pressure on the individual to conform. This can take different forms: children might face physical sanctions and adults would definitely face verbal admonishing from several family elders. In the worst case scenarios, individuals could be ostracised. On the positive side, the pressure brought to bear by the group can act as a constructive force, for instance by dissuading individuals from anti-social behaviour. The extended family also helps to maintain social unity, for example by intervening to bring about a resolution to family disputes and grievances, and marital difficulties between couples.

A significant consequence of the need within the culture to maintain the status quo is that it breeds a dislike of change. Nothing says this better than the Yoruba adage *Ẹ jẹ́ kí a ṣé bí wọ́n ṣe ńṣeé, kí o ba leèrí bí ó ṣe ńrí,* which translated means 'let us continue to do it as it has always been done, so that it can be as it has always been'. Accompanying the dislike for change is a strong fear of the unknown leading to an element of risk avoidance. Exuberant and boisterous activities by young people are frowned upon for fear that they may lead to danger. When children are injured through such activities despite warnings to dissuade them, adults will often make comments such as *Şé ojú ẹ ti já? Kí lo wá lọ? Oun tí ojú ẹ ńwá lojú ẹ rí,* which translated loosely means 'Are you satisfied with the outcomes of your foray?', 'What were you looking for?' (meaning why could you not stay within the boundaries we outlined for you?), 'You've got what you deserved'. These sayings sound harsh, but are designed to discourage such forays in future. Yoruba children in British schools, particularly boys, are likely to be more boisterous during playtimes as cultural conditioning will have discouraged such behaviour at home. They are also less likely to be able to gauge risk to themselves, and possibly others, since this function would have been carried out by parents.

Close family networking and extended family links mean that hospitality is a core value. Most Yoruba families living in Britain will play host to a range of relatives and kinsmen on a regular basis. This may have implications for children's privacy, especially when they are teenagers. It can also cause overcrowding, at least by British standards. The vast majority of first and second generation Yoruba people living in Britain carry significant financial responsibilities for their extended families back in Nigeria. Many of them, therefore, work long hours and sometimes hold two or more jobs to make ends meet. This reduces the amount of quality time available to spend with their children. The absence of the extended family to support, as would have happened were they living in Nigeria, means many of these children may not have sufficient interaction with adults to guide their thinking and views in general.

Gender Roles

In Yoruba culture, men are considered to be the head of the home and enjoy a higher status than women. Nonetheless, Yoruba women enjoy a much higher status than their counterparts in most of the other Nigerian culture groups. Older women within a family are shown the same respect as older men. Women can inherit from their fathers or husbands and many families are led by powerful matriarchs. However, a clear distinction is made between the roles that men and women play within the home. Men are expected to be the breadwinners who ensure the financial security of their families. Women are expected to help their husbands financially in whatever way they can. Many, especially those in polygamous marriages, often have to make a significant contribution to the financial resources available to raise their own children. Domestic chores are mostly carried out by women and children. Grown men are not expected to clean or cook if they have a wife. This gender bias is likely to reflect in the different expectations that parents may have of male and female children, and teenage girls living in Britain are likely to resent this. Women take on most of the day-to-day running of the family home in addition to their normal jobs, be that a professional job, farming or trading. They are also the primary caregivers for children. Fathers take on a secondary role mostly related to disciplining children for major infractions and that of counsellor as children grow older.

Marriages

Traditionally, children were expected to marry once they reached puberty. In modern times this has been deferred to when their formal education is completed. In pre-colonial times, marriages were often arranged on behalf of children. While this practice is not completely dead, in modern times, most young people find their own spouses. Nonetheless, there is still a tendency for parents to want their children to marry within the culture group and certainly to someone they approve of. Indeed, sometimes, parents may disapprove of their children marrying people from other Yoruba tribes. This is a leftover from the Yoruba civil wars which engulfed the major city states in the late 1800s and heralded colonial rule.

Once families approve their children's prospective spouses, the marriage transaction is carried out, not just between the couple, but also between their two families. A series of ceremonies are conducted over a period of time, and in some cases within a very short period. These ceremonies serve to introduce the families to each other and acknowledge the giving away of a bride to the groom's family. Traditionally, these would have been the wedding ceremonies and are currently legally recognised in Nigeria as marriage 'by native law and custom'. In modern times, civil or religious ceremonies are usually conducted in addition, usually after the traditional ceremonies. Civil marriages conducted without the traditional ceremonies usually do not enjoy the same recognition within families as those that are.

Marriages are expected to produce children to carry on the family line. It is considered a great sorrow for a couple to remain childless, and many polygamous marriages are a result of, what is often thought to be, the woman's failure to bear children. Yoruba culture cannot comprehend the idea of people choosing not to have children. The very notion is an anathema. While parents will rejoice equally at the birth of a child, be it male or female, there is still an innate desire by most men to produce a son to carry on the family name. Where a woman bears only female children, men may seek to produce a son through polygamy.

The Role of Children

Since conformity and compliance are highly valued, parents work hard at ensuring their children think and behave as part of a group. Children are taught to obey social conventions from a very young age. Those who are strong-willed or argumentative may be sanctioned heavily to discourage such traits. Adults would frown upon children asking the question 'why', particularly where this questions authority or pushes people to explain their actions. In more traditional and less educated families, children will be admonished if they interrupt adult conversations with opinions of their own without being asked.

From an early age, parents will start preparing their

children for adult roles. Children are expected to learn from adults by observing what they do. Children as young as five will share family chores such as sweeping or fetching things for adults. As they grow older and stronger, they will be encouraged to take on other duties such as cleaning and cooking, first by working alongside older people and eventually on their own. Older siblings will look after younger ones in the absence of their parents. Where necessary, they will also have responsibility for helping the elderly within the family. First born children tend to be natural leaders as they are raised as the 'elders' of their generation within the family. Those living in Britain are therefore likely to have more family responsibilities than their peers from other cultural backgrounds. For example, the expectation to look after their younger siblings will be a norm even though they may be quite young themselves.

Chapter 4:

Attitudes to Child-rearing and Education

Ilé lèniyàn ti ńkẹ̀ṣọ́ ròde

(People learn to be fashionable from home)

Child-rearing Practices

Communal child rearing practices are the norm in Yoruba land. The close proximity of the extended family means all can lend a helping hand in raising a child. When a child is born, older females within the family will come to help the new mother, who is not expected to do much work for the first forty days. There is plenty of support and advice for the new mother during this period. Most babies will be fed on demand and mother and child routines are not as regimented or structured as is often seen in Britain. Later on, older siblings and other female family members will help with babysitting and other chores.

As babies become toddlers they will play with and learn from other children within the community. There are no structured bed times and children will usually fall asleep after their evening meal whenever they are tired. In rural communities, grandparents and the elderly will often gather the young children around them in the evening and engage them in storytelling and songs. This routine, sometimes called *Tales by Moonlight*, was a common practice in pre-modern times, but is less common now, especially in urban areas. The tales and fables usually had a moral and were used as the earliest means of transmitting cultural values and norms to children. In many ways, this is comparable to the British practice of reading bedtime stories to children.

Adults try to preserve the innocence of young children for as long as possible and especially avoid answering questions pertaining to life and death. Instead, adults will tell inquisitive children fables or happy stories to answer their questions. For example, a child inquiring after a dead person may be told the person in question has travelled to a faraway place of great beauty. Rather than telling them not to do things, children will be taught about unacceptable practices through myths and fables. For example, to encourage children to sit down and eat properly at mealtimes, they will be told that eating standing up will cause the food to go straight to their legs. As no child wants fat legs and an empty stomach, they will be quick to comply!

Within the confines of the family compound and the extended family, children are free to roam and play. However, since adults are quite protective of the young, venturing beyond the immediate vicinity is often discouraged. As children grow older and begin to go to school by themselves or with other siblings or children within the community, this is reinforced through the very strict time allowances made for travel between school and the home.

Attitudes to Education

The Yoruba culture recognises the importance of the role of the family in inculcating good values in children so that they grow up to be morally upright citizens. The family takes responsibility for the child's social and cultural education, while schools are expected to be responsible for their intellectual education. Yoruba parents almost always have very high aspirations for their children.

Providing children with a good all-round education is extremely important, as this is seen as a ladder towards upward social mobility.

Parents usually have definitive ideas of what profession they would like their children to enter and these may not necessarily coincide with either their child's aptitudes or interests. 'White collar' jobs and careers are deemed more desirable as they are synonymous with the higher classes. At the same time, education is also seen as a means of equipping the individual to become a useful member of the group. This is quite distinct from what happens in the western hemisphere, where education is seen as a tool for equipping individuals to make life choices and decisions to ensure their self-reliance. Parents who have built business empires may want their children to follow careers which will help to consolidate their wealth, a notion not uncommon among the higher echelons of British society. Others may want their children to take over their businesses and therefore want them to take courses to this end. For other parents, having well-educated and highly qualified children helps to raise their own social status within the community. As such, young people may face significant pressure and find themselves in conflict with their parents when it comes to making career choices.

Discipline Methods

The culture's approach to behaviour management relies heavily on the use of punitive discipline methods to discourage poor behaviour. Although children can be praised for being good, the use of positive behaviour modification strategies to promote good behaviour is not the norm. Children can be admonished or corrected by any adult within the community. While minor infractions would usually attract a verbal rebuke, serious offences attract physical forms of punishment such as caning or repetitive physical exertion such as squats. Physical forms of punishment are usually only applied by parents and guardians, although any adult can admonish verbally.

Yoruba children are forbidden to look directly at anyone who is admonishing them. The expected body language would be for the child to look down in submission. Direct eye contact is considered to be extremely rude and represents a direct challenge to authority. Children learn this rule very early and will follow it even within a school context. This contrasts starkly with the British expectation that children should look at the adults who are talking to them.

There are checks and balances within the system to mitigate against physical abuse. Other family members, and even neighbours, can intervene on behalf of a child about to be disciplined. By doing so, they make themselves jointly liable for the child's future conduct. The child also becomes accountable to these adults for his or her behaviour in future. Such intervention could lead to either a reduction in the punishment or its deferment, subject to good conduct in future. The intervening adults would check on the child's behaviour frequently thereafter. In order to attract as many defenders as possible, smart children learn to cry loudly when they know corporal punishment is imminent!

As physical punishment is meant to correct and not abuse a child, the culture encourages adults not to apply it when they are very angry. Thus when the punishment is administered, it can be done in a measured manner. This is expressed in the saying *Wọn kìí namọ tó bá da epo nù, ọjọ́ tó bá da omi nù, á jìyà ẹ̀ pọ̀,* meaning 'you do not beat the child who has just spilled expensive oil.

The day he spills water, his sanction can take account of his previous negligence'. Another saying, *Tí a bá fi ọwọ́ òsì bá ọmọ wí, ǎfi ọwọ́ ọ̀tún fǎ mọ́ra*, meaning 'after beating your child with your left hand, you should draw him close or embrace him with your right hand', reflects the need to both admonish and encourage.

IMPLICATIONS FOR BRITISH SCHOOLS

Chapter 5:

Potential Areas of Cultural Conflict in School

Yoruba Children Transferring to British Schools

The Nigerian national curriculum, particularly at primary school level, covers a narrower number of subjects with a strong focus on basic literacy and numeracy skills. The curriculum is content based, with a heavy emphasis on subject matter rather than skills and application. Children, even the very bright ones, who transfer between the two systems, especially from Nigeria to Britain, may find the changes very difficult to cope with. Children who have experienced this talk about how demoralised and confused they were, moving from being at the top of their class in Nigeria to being in the third or bottom sets in Britain. Those who have been used to rote learning find they have to acquire a different set of learning skills in order to be successful. By not understanding the child's educational background, schools can sometimes misjudge a child's needs and aptitude, and by placing him or her in the wrong learning group can trigger disaffection. It is therefore imperative that schools do not take their initial assessment of such pupils' abilities at face value and should check carefully to ensure the right provision is made for their needs.

The transition can be just as confusing for parents. Those who do not understand the differences in the education systems sometimes consider the British education system to be inferior. This is because they often measure their children's progress by how much factual knowledge they have acquired, particularly in English and mathematics. Given the broader range of subjects that pupils study in Britain, the initial knowledge gained in English and mathematics may appear to be less than that of their peers in Nigeria, and parents may mistake this as lack of progress.

Children's Attitudes to Learning

For children of Yoruba descent, early childhood conditioning to think as part of a group may have a significant impact on their thought processes. This would be more apparent in British schools where children are expected to think as individuals. Group thinking encourages individuals to seek solutions to their problems from others within the group, rather than rely on self-ingenuity. Children raised within the culture may be good team players but may need encouragement to be more adventurous or self-reliant. Some are likely to voice the thoughts and ideas of others or what they think adults and teachers want to hear, not because they are incapable of individual thought, but because they have been socialised differently. In British classrooms some children, especially where they have had their initial schooling in Nigeria, may need to learn that it is acceptable to say what they really think.

Use of English as an Additional Language

Many Yoruba children living in Britain face the issue of language loss. English is the official language used in politics, commerce and education in Nigeria. The majority of Nigerians will learn at least a rudimentary form of English and most will speak English to a high degree of proficiency. The colonial status of English and its use as a national unifier (Nigeria has several hundred languages and dialects) means that the language often enjoys a higher status than the native languages. The ability to use the language well reflects status and a higher level of education. Certainly, for most of the last forty years, the use of native languages was forbidden during school hours in most secondary schools in Nigeria. In many middle and upper class Yoruba families, people speak both languages fluently and often move in and out of both within the same sentence. This practice has become entrenched over the last five decades as it is easier to use English derivatives of modern words, particularly those related to technology, than it is to invent a Yoruba descriptor. Indeed, many people are unable to speak conversational Yoruba without at some point having to resort to the use of English words. As a result, many Yoruba children living in Britain may not have extensive opportunities to be exposed to or use the language.

This phenomenon is complicated by the fact that most Nigerian children in Britain prefer not to use their native language even when their parents encourage its use. This is mainly due to their desire to fit in with the mainstream culture group. Unless parents enforce the use of Yoruba at home, many children grow up without being able to speak the language. Even those who learnt to speak it in Nigeria before moving to Britain often lose it due to disuse.

For these reasons, it is not unusual for Nigerians registering their children in schools to indicate that their children speak only English. Schools are sometimes perplexed and irritated by this, particularly as this can affect funding for supporting children who speak English as an additional language. It might be useful to explain to parents that although their children, especially the youngest, may speak conversational English with a relatively high degree of fluency, it usually takes longer for pupils to understand the deeper nuances of the language. They may, therefore, still require additional support in school, particularly with their comprehension, inference and deduction skills.

Child-rearing Practices

Yoruba parents living in the UK miss the extended family support so readily available in Nigeria and therefore find child-rearing more labour intensive. The obligation to provide financial support to extended relatives living back home often means that mothers cannot afford to take time off work and stay home to raise their children. The high cost of living in Britain and expensive childcare often leads to mothers returning to work without the ability to provide appropriate alternative childcare. Therefore, children may sometimes be left on their own or with older siblings who, by British standards, may not necessarily be old enough to look after them. This can put children at risk and can get parents into trouble with the law.

Yoruba children living in Britain are less likely to have a specific bed time or have stories read to them before bed, as is the British norm. Parents may not understand the need to read with young children daily or due to work commitments may not be able to. Children may also go to bed late and wake up more tired than they should be. Without understanding the underlying cultural norms, British schools could interpret this as a lack of parental support for reading or neglect.

Parents may not be aware of how to use a wide range of educational resources such as museums and art galleries to support their children's learning, as these may well be outside their own cultural experiences.

Behaviour Management
The difference in the discipline methods traditionally employed by Yoruba families and those employed in British schools is the most significant area of cultural

conflict that families and schools have to negotiate. First generation immigrant Yoruba parents are more likely to use some discipline methods at home which today are generally unacceptable in Britain. While smacking is the preferred deterrent, some parents will routinely use more severe corporal punishment, mainly because they do not know how else to discipline their children. Some may not even be aware that corporal punishment is illegal in British schools. There are anecdotal stories of parents giving teachers permission to beat their children, not realising how horrifying that sounds to the average British teacher. Of course parents in these instances are simply trying to let the teachers know that they are happy to transfer their parental authority to the teachers, which would be the usual cultural norm.

Most children learn quickly to cope with the different expectations at home and school, and the vast majority adapt and conform well. However, a number of children do get mixed messages about what is acceptable, especially those just starting school. Children who are used to external deterrents to bad behaviour at home often do not respond to verbal warnings and may not even recognise that they have crossed the line at school.

Parents who are invited into school to discuss their child's misdemeanours are often frustrated at what they perceive as the school's unwillingness or inability to appropriately control their child. Often parents see this as a school problem, especially where these behaviours are not seen at home. On the other hand, having reported to parents that a child was disciplined for an offence committed at school, staff are often distressed to find that parents apply additional sanctions at home. This happens because in Yoruba culture, it is assumed that when an adult reports a child to his or her parents, the adult is saying, "*I expect you to discipline your child as I would have.*" It is therefore an expectation that the parents will act to correct the behaviour via an appropriate sanction. In addition, since the child's misdemeanour reflects badly on the child's upbringing and hence on the parents, this alone is enough to warrant additional sanctions for the 'shame' brought upon the family. To avoid these occurrences, schools need to explicitly inform parents that no further sanctions are required.

The lack of consistency in behaviour management means that some children learn to manipulate home and school much to their detriment. In most of these cases, the children behave better at home than in school, largely due to the more severe forms of discipline employed at home. Where schools suspect that discipline methods employed at home may be harsh, they are often reluctant to inform parents of minor infractions out of fear that the children could be over-disciplined. Unfortunately, when children become aware of this reluctance, their behaviour in school tends to deteriorate further until more firm measures are required. By the time this happens, parents are shocked to hear the extent of their child's bad behaviour at school and schools are equally disbelieving that parents do not see this side of their child. In most cases, it is not that the parents are in denial. They simply rarely, if ever, witness such behaviour at home. This, however, does not help home-school relations.

Where there is evidence that children are being abused physically, schools have to follow child protection procedures. This in itself usually causes deterioration in the home-school relationship. Some parents who have been cautioned about their discipline methods, and who do not have a repertoire of other behaviour management strategies, find themselves in a quandary as to how to manage their children's behaviour. This may lead to a cessation of appropriate disciplining and, inevitably, worsened behaviour.

In frustration, parents who are fearful that their children may be taken away from them by social services, or who feel incapable of managing their child's behaviour, may resort to threatening to send their child back to relatives in Nigeria, to learn '*how to behave properly*'. Indeed some do carry out this threat. This is sometimes because parents interpret the school's disapproval of the discipline methods used as giving the child license to behave as he or she pleases. Instead of hearing "*Don't discipline your child this way,*" they hear "*Don't discipline your child.*" Some see their sojourn in Britain as temporary. The fear of raising a child who is unable to fit into Yoruba society is often enough incentive to send him or her home with the hope that appropriate intervention from the extended family will improve the child's behaviour. The additional pressure put on parents to stay home and look after children that have been excluded from school also acts as a motivator in helping parents to arrive at this decision.

Schools can and do work with families successfully to modify behaviour management strategies. The key to this, as all experienced educators know, is consistency. The Yoruba culture understands this well. A common saying in the language is that you do not raise a child with 'two voices'. In this context, the 'two voices' refer to the mother and father and the saying cautions couples to ensure that they are in agreement about how to discipline their child. Without too far a stretch of the imagination, it is not difficult to translate the same saying to inconsistencies in behaviour management between home and school. Once parents see the parallel, they are very likely to cooperate fully with the school. That said, parents may still require additional support in modifying their behaviour management strategies. Schools may need to introduce parents to alternative strategies such as 'time out', withdrawal of privileges or being grounded and the use of incentives to promote good behaviour. I remember a parent who at her wits end decided to remove all her child's toys permanently. With no incentive to improve, the child's behaviour worsened. The parent was advised to withdraw some of the toys for a fixed period only and to encourage the child to earn some of them back. Needless to say the child had motivation to behave better.

Vulnerable Children and those with Special Educational Needs or Disabilities

Most Nigerian cultures, including the Yoruba, have a limited understanding of disability and its causes, and even fewer skills for coping with and supporting children with special educational needs. Children with learning needs in Nigeria are often regarded as slow, lazy or dullards and may be subject to ridicule among their peers. Despite the size of the country and its wealth, there are only a handful of special schools in Nigeria and these are mostly private schools usually accessible only to wealthier families. In rural settings, physical disability is often surrounded by many religious taboos linked to animism and may be regarded as a punishment from the gods, a result of some unwholesome activity carried out by the parents or a result of black magic against the family. Even in Christian circles, behavioural and learning difficulties may be attributed to spiritual influences and demonic activity.

Some of the cultural responses and taboos attached to disability can be linked to the collectivist nature of the culture. Given that Yoruba society derives its strength from the group, the worth of each individual is often defined by what they are able to contribute to ensure the well-being, success and security of the group. With few structures to support the effective education or rehabilitation of people with special needs and the absence of a state sponsored welfare system, such people become the burden and responsibility of extended family. In addition to this, the lack of easy access to modern medicine, science or research for the majority of people, means that religious explanations may be found for medical conditions, and the Yoruba are deeply religious.

While children with special needs living in Britain obviously have access to much more than their counterparts in the developing world, centuries of ingrained taboos and prejudices mean that many Yoruba parents living in Britain are less likely to accept that their child has a disability, thereby making it difficult for the child to receive the additional support they are entitled to. Yoruba parents in Britain almost always give a negative response when schools suggest their child might have special educational needs. Parents will often deny there is a problem or hope that a range of spiritual or medical remedies will provide a cure. Without parental cooperation schools find it difficult, if not impossible, to secure appropriate funding and help for children with special needs. One of the major reasons for denial and the refusal to accept disability is the fear that the child will not be able to grow into a productive adult. Therefore, the more schools can show parents examples of successful and productive people living with disability within society, the more likely they are to allay parents' fears and secure their cooperation.

Welfare Issues

In the 1950s and 60s, Nigerian parents studying in Britain usually had their children privately fostered. As self-supporting students who studied during the day and worked in the evenings or at night, most could not afford live-in child care. Yet deferring parenthood was not a cultural option. The solution was to send their children to live with foster parents who were paid to look after children full time. This was probably viewed as an extension to the cultural practice of children being raised by other family members. Children of school age would spend their holidays with their parents but lived full time with their foster parents. Siblings, however, were not always fortunate enough to live with the same foster parent. This practice diminished significantly in the late 1980s and 1990s. However, these days, children may still find themselves in the care of older siblings or people who are not blood relatives, particularly when parents need to leave the country suddenly due to a death in the family. For most children, this is very brief, but there have been known instances of children living without their parents for extended periods. This often happens with parents with immigration issues who have difficulty getting back into Britain.

Illegal immigration, a perennial problem in Britain, also has welfare implications for some children. Where parents are illegal immigrants, children sometimes experience poverty which is well hidden. A classic symptom tends to be parents who do not pay for their children's meals but refuse offers to claim for benefits and avoid interaction with school authorities.

Another less common practice is that of bringing adolescents from the extended family into Britain, as dependants to support child care needs. While most are well looked after, some of these young people are vulnerable to exploitation, physical abuse, neglect or domestic drudgery. While the signs are easy enough to spot: unwillingness or refusal to take part in activities out of school hours, excessive tiredness, incomplete homework, reticence, malnourishment and unkemptness, to mention a few; it is extremely difficult to prove. The children are usually fearful of being returned to poverty in Africa and the displeasure of their own families. In some cases, they may not be living with relatives at all. Instead they may be indentured servants whose families have already been paid large amounts of money in advance for their services. As such, they are less likely to cooperate with school authorities. Dealing with such cases requires sensitivity, particularly in relation to the child's needs.

Parental Involvement

Educators acknowledge that the educational experience of most parents is likely to be very different from that of their children. For parents who were educated in Nigeria, this is doubly so. Teaching methods in Nigeria are very different. The failure of successive Nigerian governments to adequately fund the education system over the past two decades has left the vast majority of schools lacking in basic resources and the technological infrastructure so often taken for granted in British schools. Nigerian schools therefore have to adapt their teaching methods to suit their context, which makes for very didactic teaching and extremely large classrooms. The sheer size of classes means that teaching tends to lean towards the middle ability pupil with little or no adjustment to meet the varying needs of others. Children who fail to keep pace with the class are usually left behind. Consequently, they may be required to repeat the year as often as it takes to achieve a pass grade before moving up to the next year group.

It is therefore likely that very few first time parents will be aware of how mixed ability classes work in British schools or how teachers plan lessons so that work is matched to pupils' individual needs and abilities. In my experience as an educator, parents have been known to request that their child be held back a year when the child's performance is below age-related expectations. Parents are often confused when schools refuse to do this and they may question the school's ability to meet their child's needs. Explaining how the British school system works is therefore useful for such parents.

In Nigeria, there is a distinct separation between work and play, and children in the Early Years are not taught in an integrated way. Yoruba parents are likely to have little experience or understanding of the use of play to extend children's knowledge and understanding. They may, therefore, frown upon their children's account of their school day being full of play with sand and water! On a practical note, sand does not mix very well with 'afro' hair, which is often laden with petroleum product to keep it soft and manageable. The sand tends to cling to the petroleum and the very tensile strands of hair, thus becoming impossible to get rid of. This is every African mother's worst nightmare so, often, mothers will instruct their children to avoid the sand pit. This can of course cause the child to be conflicted. A simple solution that schools can employ is to ensure that each child has their own personal shower cap for use when playing with sand.

A number of other curricular differences may also cause tension or conflict. For example, Christian parents, particularly those of Evangelical or Pentecostal persuasion, are more likely to be uncomfortable with the idea of their children visiting Sikh or Hindu temples as part of their religious education studies. The general belief tends to be that to visit such places is to open oneself to other undesirable spiritual influences. Parents may have similar opposition to their children reading literature which contains references to witchcraft in any form. This includes several books in the fantasy genre such as the *Harry Potter* series. Schools may need to consider this when stocking books and encouraging children to take them home, particularly if they have a large population of children from this religious group.

Chapter 6:

Helping Children Cope with Bi-culturalism

Most successful bi-cultural people learn the important skill of *switching* between cultures in response to appropriate cultural cues. This involves modifying one's behaviour in line with what is culturally acceptable within one's current context. For example, a Yoruba child raised in Britain and who has never been to Nigeria would kneel to greet her grandparents without being prompted. She would also refer to her parents' Nigerian friends as *uncle* or *auntie* but call their White British friends by their first name. Similarly, a teenage, British-born Nigerian male would look a policeman in the eye if being questioned, but would look down if being admonished by his father. While most children learn instinctively to switch their behaviour in response to the cultural context they find themselves in, not all learn to do this. Those who don't invariably find themselves regularly embroiled in cultural conflict of some kind. For example, Nigerian children who do not learn to modulate their voices and talk more quietly in a British cultural context often find themselves accused of aggression or shouting at school.

To be successful in life, ideally, bi-cultural people should have *integrated* bi-cultural identities. This means they would feel equally at home in any of the cultural contexts that influence their lives and would switch seamlessly in either context. Such people would feel 'comfortable in their skins' and would not be at odds with any of their cultural identities. They would therefore, for example, be happy to be either African or British when the situation requires them to do so.

However, to be able to successfully integrate one's bi-cultural identities relies heavily on the ability to switch appropriately in response to the different cultural cues. The individual who is able to switch correctly between cultural contexts experiences less cultural conflict and is therefore able to see the different cultural identities as complimentary. In contrast, individuals who are unable or unwilling to switch appropriately often experience more cultural conflict. The more this happens, the more likely they will perceive their different cultural identities as contradictory or oppositional, which in turn prevents integration. As a child growing up in Africa, and being a strong-willed individual, the art of switching did not come easily to me. As a result, I experienced conflict on a daily basis as my 'Britishness', inculcated by my White foster mother, constantly butted heads with my grandmother's African ideals. Consequently, I saw the two cultures as contradictory and for the most part longed to be back in Britain.

The more conflict an individual experiences, the more likely they are to want to 'ditch' one of their cultural identities. One response could be to discard the ethnic identity and *assimilate* into the mainstream culture. Such individuals would deny their ethnic identity and maintain a lifestyle that reflects only British culture. In my case, on my return to Britain, I refused to speak the ethnic language, wear ethnic clothing, eat ethnic food or indeed associate with anyone from the ethnic culture except for immediate family. Getting rid of my African accent was a key priority and this phase of denial went on for a number of years.

Another response could be to ignore the mainstream

culture and associate only with the ethnic culture. Technically known as *separation*, such individuals may view the mainstream culture as inferior or evil and are more prone to radicalisation and extremism. Children whose parents remain separated from the mainstream culture may come under immense pressure at home to conform to their parents' way of life. Some eventually separate from both the ethnic and mainstream cultures and create or join an alternative culture group. For Nigerian children, culturally programmed to be part of a collective, this may lead to assimilation into gang culture.

In order to avoid conflict, other children will keep each cultural identity separate and develop two personas, one usually seen at home, where the ethnic cultural influence is strongest, and one seen at school or in other social contexts outside of the ethnic culture. While this technique may help to reduce conflict for the individuals concerned, it often creates communication gaps between home and school as neither sees the child's other persona. How this may or may not affect the individual's psyche in the long run is a question for debate.

Since an individual's ability to switch successfully between cultures is often affected by the degree to which they perceive those cultures as being complementary or oppositional, it is critical that young people are helped to negotiate potential areas of cultural conflict early in life. Where children fail to learn the art of *switching* instinctively, schools should work with parents to teach them to interpret and react to cultural cues appropriately. A six year old Yoruba child attending a meeting with her teacher and mother, to discuss her previous unacceptable behaviour, is likely to face significant conflict on a deep emotional level. Her ethnic cultural expectation would demand that she hang her head in shame while being spoken to. Her teacher, on the other hand, is likely to insist that she look at her, which is the British expectation. Most children in this scenario are likely to instinctively follow the ethnic expectation, which the teacher may not understand. A simple way to help a child negotiate such a situation is for the teacher to acknowledge the cultural expectation openly and, with the parent's permission, invite the child to switch behaviour when being spoken to by the teacher.

Teenage Nigerian children who refuse to conform to their parents' cultural norms and expectations, and insist on having the same freedoms their British peers enjoy, are likely to experience significantly more cultural conflict. Helping them to develop conflict resolution strategies can go a long way in easing the transition into adulthood. Through counselling, teenagers and older children, who are at risk of rejecting their ethnic culture, can be helped to see where their own personal and moral convictions are similar to those of their ethnic culture and negotiate around those values they see as oppositional. The same is applicable to those rejecting the mainstream culture.

Creating opportunities for youngsters to research their culture more thoroughly would go a long way in improving their cultural understanding and possibly their parents' motives. Unfortunately, the content of the National Curriculum for History does not provide children with sufficient opportunity to do this. Therefore, schools may want to consider how they modify the curriculum, particularly at the primary level, to ensure that children learn as much as possible about both British and their own ethnic cultures. Children can be encouraged to use sleepovers, which they usually organise for fun, to learn something new about each other's cultures. For homework, children can be encouraged to engage in deeper research which involves their parents and other family members on the similarities and differences in the values and norms of their ethnic and mainstream cultures. Mono-cultural parents do need to understand that their children are likely to grow up being bi-cultural and will therefore have opposing views to their own. Involving whole families in such research will create opportunities for them to develop a deeper understanding of potential areas of conflict and how to avoid or minimise them.

My children once asked why I regularly called them from their bedrooms to come downstairs to get me a drink of water. Given that I was already downstairs, they could not understand why I did not simply walk into the kitchen and get it myself. I must admit that initially I was quite taken aback by the question. My Yoruba cultural response was to question my children's right to question me. However, my British identity asserted itself and recognised that I had raised my children not to go through life without asking questions. On reflection, I also realised that despite my personal conviction that I was more British than African, I had conveniently slipped into the Yoruba cultural expectation that it was my children's duty to fetch and carry for me. Following a deeper discussion about cultural roles and expectations, we agreed that I would call them less often, and they decided that they would get me a drink if they were near the kitchen even if I did not ask for one! Looking back on this many years later, what seems like a trivial event now was the beginnings of us as a family learning to negotiate on cultural expectations. Helping African parents to learn how to do this is critical.

I also remember when my daughters, around the age of eleven and thirteen, decided that my input on their clothing styles and fashion was no longer required. From then on, they wanted to be able to buy their own clothes, albeit with my money. At that time, the Evangelical African in me frowned seriously on the idea of the mini skirt which I knew they were desperate to buy. My strategy round the conflict was three-fold. First I agreed to give them a clothing allowance with which they could shop as they wished, provided certain conditions were met. I then stipulated the minimum number of items they had to purchase with the money I gave them. Finally, they were not allowed to buy skirts that were shorter than twenty-seven inches. It didn't take long for my daughters to decide that I was still trying to dress them as nuns. In the end, with a measuring tape and a little negotiation, we agreed on twenty-one inches as the minimum length. Everyone was happy. My point is, the art of negotiating with children does not come easy to Yoruba parents and whatever schools can do to help in this regard would be useful. In some instances, schools may well find that they have to broker peace between children and their parents.

The Yoruba parents' tendency towards being overprotective of their young means that many children do not learn to do their own risk assessments, which makes them even more vulnerable to harm, be it from drugs, unprotected sex, or gang culture. Parents are likely to try to dissuade, if not forbid, their children from going to pubs, parties and anything else the children might consider fun. Helping children and parents to understand each other's motives and encouraging parents to allow children to manage their own risks can help in negotiating around some of these issues. My children eventually learnt, when seeking permission to go to such events, to allay my fears by explaining what they had done or planned to do to alleviate any potential risks. Although they may give different reasons for their refusal, some parents refuse to allow their children to go on school organised residential trips out of fear. Where this happens, in order to allay their fears, schools may find it worthwhile to explain to parents at great length all the actions they have taken to minimise the risks to their children.

Improving Home–School Relationships

Clearly, a better understanding of each other's norms and values would enable teachers and parents to work effectively together to provide children with the best support possible. The key to a successful relationship between schools and parents is a well thought out induction programme at the time a child starts school. The induction programme for Yoruba families should cover a wide range of issues including cultural ones with a potential to cause tension. Topics should include behaviour management strategies at home and school, and child protection triggers and procedures. If possible, parents should be given opportunities to discuss discipline methods used at home and, where appropriate, be introduced to alternative or supplementary methods. These can be done, for example, during home visits which many Early Years practitioners conduct before a child starts school.

Parents should also be alerted to the negative effect that taking holidays in term time can have on children's achievement. Most local authorities provide schools with statistics which show the correlation between poor attendance and attainment. Sharing this information with parents and discussing these issues during the induction process will enable families to make more informed choices. While parents may have little or no control over funerals and when they take place, much control can be exercised over dates for family weddings. Since weddings are family contracts, usually, key family players and not just the couple will be involved in choosing dates. If a wedding is important enough for a family to travel from Britain to Nigeria, they will most certainly be key players and may therefore have some jurisdiction over the timing.

Many schools hold annual social days for children and their parents to celebrate culture and diversity. These useful events tend to focus mostly on the minority ethnic cultures and schools do not always fully exploit the potential to share something of British culture as well.

The work commitments of many parents may prevent them from attending important school meetings organised in the evenings or during school hours. Yoruba people love social functions and will usually turn out for weekend events. As a headteacher, I learnt to sandwich important parents' meetings in-between social events, which included performances by the children. I would let a few classes, usually the older ones, perform first. This meant parents would not disappear with the younger children before the end of the event. I would then make a short presentation on whatever the topic was while I had a captive audience, before allowing the rest of the festivities to continue. It worked every time.

Another thing to note is that within Britain there are no established community leaders for the African communities, as happens in some of the Asian minority groups. This role is usually vested in church or other religious leaders. Schools may therefore find it useful to use the main religious organisations within their locality as a point of contact on cultural issues. I have worked with pastors who have been willing to allow me to give short talks to parents right after, or in some cases, instead of, the Sunday sermon. While these strategies might sound unusual, the point to remember is that in the long run they benefit all concerned, particularly the children. Parents should, however, at all times be given advance notice of such activities and if possible advance notice of the programme of events. This ensures that their right to exercise choice is not taken away.

Chapter 7:

Conclusion

In this book I have tried to explain that cultural values influence how people behave and how they interpret experiences, including educational ones. Different cultures may share common as well as distinct and opposing values. For bi-cultural individuals who operate in and out of cultures that have opposing values, this will generate an element of cultural conflict. Most people, irrespective of their cultural background, manage some form of cultural conflict successfully on a daily basis without being conscious that they are doing so. However, for some individuals, the conflict brings about such intense negative emotional stress that it affects their ability to integrate successfully within society. For young bi-cultural individuals, this presents an element of challenge for both the individuals and their schools. Schools therefore need to be better informed about the norms and values of their minority ethnic groups so that they can serve the children and their families better.

A Case in Point

*** *Primary School is an inner London three-form entry school, situated in an area where sixty percent of the community is from a Yoruba cultural heritage. The school runs an induction programme over two evenings for new parents which includes discussions about behaviour management, child protection, homework, bedtime routines as well as the school's expectations of how it would like parents to support its work. At the end of the second session, parents are asked to sign a home-school agreement which staff explain in great detail.*

Last year, the school noticed that several children of Yoruba heritage were regularly picked up late after school. Some of these had to wait for parents to finish at work and some had to wait for their older siblings who attended the local secondary school. Some of the same children were left in the playground by their parents very early in the morning, well before most of the staff arrived. The school sent numerous letters home to the specific parents to encourage them to pick up their children earlier and not to leave them unsupervised in the playground in the mornings, but these had no impact. The school consulted a local church pastor in order to develop a better understanding of the issues that faced the community. They found out that several of the parents in question were single mothers who held early morning cleaning jobs. This was the main reason why their children were left in the playground too early. Coming from a culture where children were expected to have high levels of responsibility early in life, the parents did not see any harm in leaving the children in the playground to look after themselves. The pastor also found out that one of the parents did not work and was considering becoming a childminder but did not know how to go about doing this. The school agreed to support this parent in gathering all the information needed in order to register as a childminder. They also supported her through the registration process. Once she was registered, the pastor worked with and encouraged the other parents to use the childminder's services to look after the children in the morning.

Some of the children who were left late in the evening had a similar issue because their parents were unable to leave work early enough to collect them at the end of the school day. While this issue was resolved for those who used the services of the new childminder, it still left a few pupils with no adequate provision. Although the school ran an after-school club, their parents did not use it because they could not afford to. The school agreed to reduce the cost of using this facility for those parents, and the church also made a generous donation towards the school's costs, thereby making it more affordable for the parents. A portion of the school's fundraising proceeds were set aside to help needy families access other provisions, such as school residential trips, that they might otherwise not be able to afford. To develop closer links with the community, when a community governor vacancy arose, the school worked hard to ensure that it was filled by someone from the Yoruba cultural background. This ensured that the governing body had some representation from the community.

In discussion with her class, the Year 3 teacher found out that none of her pupils had ever been into a local museum which was literally ten minutes from the school. The museum had an exhibition of ancient Yoruba and Benin artefacts and masks which would greatly enhance the history topic on Ancient Benin. To generate pupils' enthusiasm for the topic, the teacher held a Saturday morning workshop for the pupils and their parents at the museum. Most of the parents had never seen these artefacts before and were very interested to see some of the ancient art from their home country. They did not realise such a facility existed within the community or that their children could derive much enjoyment and learning from visiting one. Many informed the teacher that they would visit the museum often in the future. On the other hand, a small group of parents had strong reservations about their children being exposed to what they considered to be artefacts of a 'pagan' nature, and were not happy that they had not been informed beforehand that this was what they would see at the museum.

On her return to school, the teacher discussed her experience with the headteacher. It was decided from then on that the museum would be invited to send a representative to the induction meetings for new parents, to introduce them to the museum. It was agreed that future visits to the museum would make clear to parents the nature of the exhibition so that those who wished to opt out on religious grounds could do so. Subsequently, the school decided to put together an information pack of similar facilities in the neighbourhood for all existing parents. They also considered periodically inviting the different organisations to parents' meetings held in school as a means of introducing parents to these facilities. ★★★

The case study above shows how a school could work with its local community to develop more effective support for the children and families it serves. Schools can do much to support the cultural integration of bi-cultural individuals by taking appropriate steps to understand the cultures they are working with and by working closely with parents and other community agencies. Indeed many already do, although not always from a good understanding of the needs of the cultures they are working with. This book represents that first step in relation to getting to know the Yoruba culture. I hope the insights provided will help teachers and educators who work with children of Yoruba descent and their families to understand and better provide for their needs.

Acknowledgements

I am grateful to all the people who read the initial manuscript, and whose feedback helped to shape my thoughts: Kekshan Salaria, Deji and Dotun Okubadejo, Holly Broughton, Tola Okogwu, Dele and Vivien Oke, and Seye Olajide. I would also like to thank my family for their support, encouragement, and for allowing me to use our 'life stories' in this book. Special thanks go to Jola, our cover model. Finally to my husband, Dele, I say a big thank you for the 'not so gentle' promptings, which gave me the courage to write book.